AF322686

To :
Jace, Zoe, Raegan, Ryleigh

In every phase of your life remember to work with all your heart & don't forget to be patient, kind, loving, good, gentle, faithful, joyful, calm, and disciplined.
Auntie Loves You

"The fruit of the Spirit is love, joy, peace,
forbearance, kindness, goodness,
faithfulness, gentleness, and self- control"
Galatians 5:22-23

Every Spring we visit my grandma Maggie.
She lives in a beautiful home surrounded with trees.

Almost every tree was planted by grandma herself!

Grandma Maggie loves to garden.
She always says . . .
"whatever you do, work at it with all your heart!"
And she really does!

Although everything grandma plants seems to take a million
years to grow. . .
She always gardens with a smile on her face.
She never gets tired of the process or the results.

Magnolia
Seeds
Magnolia
Seeds
Magnolia
Seeds
Magnolia
Seeds

I want to be like grandma. That's why this year I've decided to plant my own tree.
Yes, in fact,
I will plant a Magnolia tree.

Grandma Maggie says
"Magnolia trees take a lot of time and devotion, are you sure
you're ready for this?"

I smile at her and say

"I'm ready"

Grandma says the first step is to love the seed with all your heart because whatever you love you will take care of.

Ha! Too easy for me, I love Magnolia trees
Check and done!

Grandma says the next step is to find joy in finding the perfect spot to plant our seed.
This was TOO EASY.
Grandma helped me find the perfect spot and we laughed the entire time!

Grandma says that this next step is easy for anyone who loves.

Now you have to be kind, calm, and gentle when placing the seed into the ground"

Grandma looks at me smiling and says "these next steps are for you to do on your own, I will be here to support you, but you have to do this so that like your tree, you too will grow."

You must be patient and consistent in order to see your tree bloom into something beautiful. No matter how long it takes, whatever you do, work at it with all your heart."

And I did!
Every year that we went to grandma's I would rush out to water, talk to, and take care of our magnolia tree.

But year after year...

AFTER YEAR...

Our Magnolia tree was still as tiny as can be.

But I remembered the words of my grandmother
You must be patient and consistent in order to see your tree
bloom into something beautiful, no matter how long it takes."

So I waited and remained patient and consistent.

Several years passed and grandma Maggie was gone.

But there stood our beautiful Magnolia tree covered in pink and white magnolias.

Love

Joy

Kind, Calm, Gentle

Patience, Consistency

Self-discipline

Because of grandma Maggie I not only love to garden but I now know the importance of having

ove, peace, joy, kindness, goodness, gentleness, consistency, patience, and self discipline.

I will never get tired of the process or the result of
Our Magnolia Tree.

The End.